629.45 WIL

TWENTY NAMES IN SPACE EXPLORATION

Williams, Brian Discarded

DEMCO

# Twenty
## Names In
# Space Exploration

Brian Williams

Illustrated by Peter Dennis

MARSHALL CAVENDISH
New York · London · Toronto · Sydney

**Editor:** Sarah Doughty
**Consultant Editor:** Maggi McCormick

# Reference Edition published 1990

© Marshall Cavendish Limited 1990
© Wayland (Publishers) Limited 1989

Published by Marshall Cavendish Corporation
147, West Merrick Road
Freeport
Long Island
N.Y. 11520

**Library of Congress Cataloging-in-Publication Data**

Williams, Brian
  Twenty names in space exploration / Brian Williams : illustrated by
Peter Dennis.
      p. cm. – (Twenty names)
  Includes bibliographical references.
  Summary: Brief biographies of twenty important space scientists and
astronauts.
  ISBN 1-85435-256-3
  1. Astronauts – Biography – Juvenile literature. 2. Astronauts -
Bibliography – Juvenile literature. [1. Astronautics. 2. Astronauts.] I.
Dennis, Peter,, ill. II. Title. III. Title: 20 names in space exploration. IV.
Series.
TL789.85.A1W55 1989
629.45'0092'2-dc20
[B]                                                            89-23901
[920]                                                              CIP
                                                                   AC

Printed in Italy by G. Canale & C. S.p.A., Turin.

# Contents

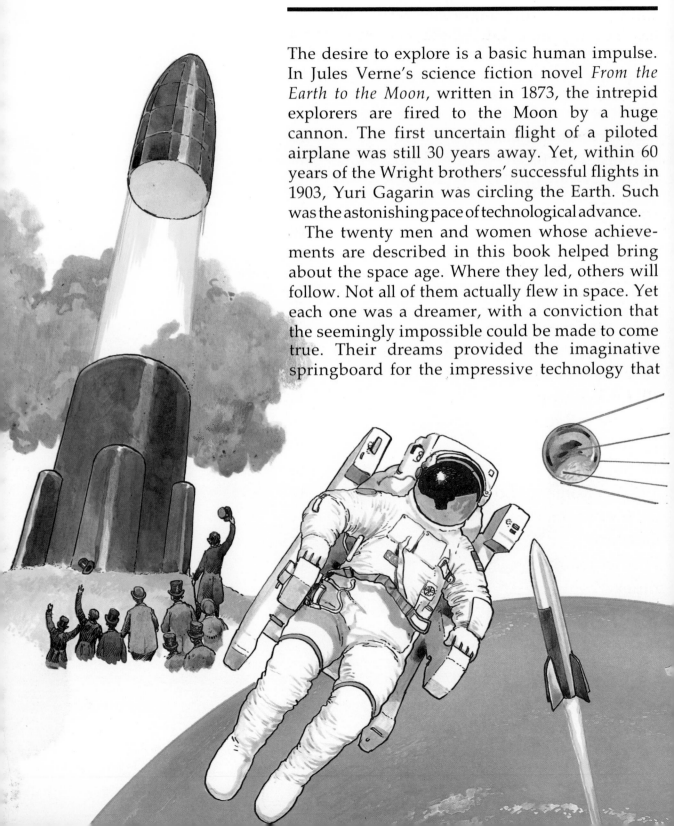

# From Visions to Voyages

The desire to explore is a basic human impulse. In Jules Verne's science fiction novel *From the Earth to the Moon*, written in 1873, the intrepid explorers are fired to the Moon by a huge cannon. The first uncertain flight of a piloted airplane was still 30 years away. Yet, within 60 years of the Wright brothers' successful flights in 1903, Yuri Gagarin was circling the Earth. Such was the astonishing pace of technological advance.

The twenty men and women whose achievements are described in this book helped bring about the space age. Where they led, others will follow. Not all of them actually flew in space. Yet each one was a dreamer, with a conviction that the seemingly impossible could be made to come true. Their dreams provided the imaginative springboard for the impressive technology that springboard for the impressive technology that has taken people into space and sent robot spacecraft voyaging beyond our solar system.

Space exploration is a very costly business. Its critics argue that the expense in unjustifiable when so much remains to be done on Earth. Its supporters point to the benefits: weather forecasting by satellite, improved communications and mapping, and global resource management. Military uses of space remain a key and controversial area.

Space will never be "conquered." That we venture beyond our planet at all is a triumph of invention brought about by a partnership of engineers and scientists, technicians and astronauts. All exploration involves risk, and the loss of the space shuttle *Challenger*, blown up in full view of the world's television cameras in 1986, reminds us of the perils that await every voyager into space.

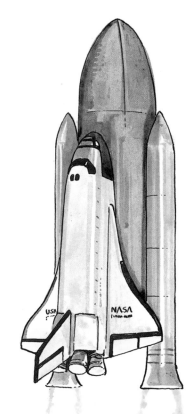

# 1
# Konstantin Tsiolkovski

The Russian scientist, Konstantin Tsiolkovski, dreamed of a day when people would fly in space. Unlike the science fiction writers of his day, he actually worked out the theoretical basis for spaceflight technology.

Childhood deafness, followed by the death of his mother when he was 13, left Tsiolkovski lonely, but self-reliant. He had a passion for reading, and he became a dedicated student of science and mathematics. While he was a student in Moscow, he worked for such long hours that his father feared he would make himself ill and ordered him to come home.

Tsiolkovski worked as a school teacher. He also married and raised a family. He lived quietly, hardly ever meeting other scientists. When he sent the results of some research to the famous chemist, Dmitri Mendeleyev, he received a friendly letter regretting that the research had

already been done, 25 years earlier.

However, Mendeleyev encouraged Tsiolkovski to go on with his work. Tsiolkovski built a wind tunnel to test the design of a new all-metal airship. He designed flying machines, years before the Wright brothers made the first "heavier-than-air" flight in 1903.

In 1895, he wrote a book called *Dreams of Earth and Sky* about space travel. He pondered on how people could communicate with extraterrestrial beings. His greatest book is called *Exploration of Cosmic Space by means of Reaction Devices*. Reaction devices meant rockets. Tsiolkovski realized that only rocket power would enable people to break free of gravity and enter space. By his writings, he inspired others to build such rockets.

Little notice was taken of Tsiolkovski's work until after the 1917 Russian Revolution. He died in 1935, before the first jet plane had flown. One hundred years after his birth, in 1957, the Russians launched Sputnik 1, and the space age began.

| | |
|---|---|
| **1857** | born at Izhevskoye, Russia |
| **1866** | becomes deaf as a result of illness |
| **1874** | studies science in Moscow |
| **1876** | starts work as a school teacher |
| **1893** | builds wind tunnel to test airship design |
| **1895** | writes book about space travel |
| **1896** | speculates on the likelihood of life on distant planets |
| **1902** | flood destroys home and laboratory |
| **1917** | Russian Revolution |
| **1919** | elected to the Academy of Sciences |
| **1921** | granted life pension by government |
| **1935** | dies |

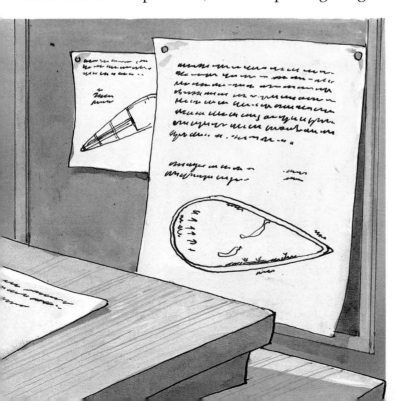

*Tsiolkovski turned the visions of his imagination into sketches and technical specifications for spacecraft.*

# 2
# Robert Goddard

Robert Hutchings Goddard is often called the "father of the American space program," even though he died in 1945 – long before an American rocket big enough to fly into space even existed.

Goddard became interested in space flight while he was a student at home in Worcester, Massachusetts. This interest grew stronger after he became a university professor. Goddard advocated research into rockets, and the Smithsonian Institution provided him with funds and published his work.

At first, Goddard experimented with solid fuels (like those in fireworks rockets), but soon he switched to liquid fuels. His was a lonely path to follow, for there were few others with whom he could share ideas.

In 1926, Goddard tested the world's first liquid-fueled rocket. His rockets were small, rising only

| | |
|---|---|
| **1882** | born Worcester, Massachusetts |
| **1911** | doctorate at Clark University |
| **1914** | professor of physics at Clark (until 1943) |
| **1919** | funded to do rocket research |
| **1926** | test-fires first liquid-fueled rocket |
| **1930s** | suggests that multi-stage rockets would be needed to escape Earth's gravity |
| **1935** | builds a rocket that exceeds the speed of sound |
| **1941** | Goddard designs rocket motors for aircraft |
| **1945** | dies |

*Robert Goddard stands beside the launching platform which holds his rocket.*

a few hundred yards, but they worked. He traveled to the New Mexico desert to find better conditions, working out how such rockets could be controlled in flight by gyroscopes.

Goddard was sure that rockets would work better in the vacuum of space than in air. He suggested that a rocket made up of several stages could, in theory, reach the Moon. Most people considered him a crank, one more mad professor. But some took notice, and Goddard's ideas were used by the Germans to develop their V2 rocket.

During World War II, Goddard worked on military projects for the U.S. Air Force in Maryland. He died as the war came to an end. Had he lived a few months longer, he might have met Wernher von Braun and the other German rocket scientists after the war. The country paid the quiet professor a belated tribute in 1962, when the Goddard Space Flight Center in Maryland was dedicated in his honor.

**Above** *A desert test-firing of Goddard's liquid-fueled rocket.*

# 3
# Hermann Oberth

Had his father's wish prevailed, Hermann Oberth would have been a doctor of medicine, not a visionary pioneer of rocketry. Oberth was born in what was then the Austro-Hungarian Empire, but he later became a German citizen. While studying medicine, he managed to fit in extra classes in math and astronomy, and he became an amateur rocket designer.

During World War I (1914–18), Oberth was wounded, and while recovering, he sketched plans for a long-range liquid-fueled rocket. Oberth was a member of the Army Medical Corps, and his commanding officer was impressed with his work. He sent the plans to the War Ministry, but they were rejected as "pure fantasy."

Oberth was to encounter similar scepticism as he pursued his dream. He gave up medicine to study spaceflight technology. He wrote a book about his rocket, but no one would publish it. So

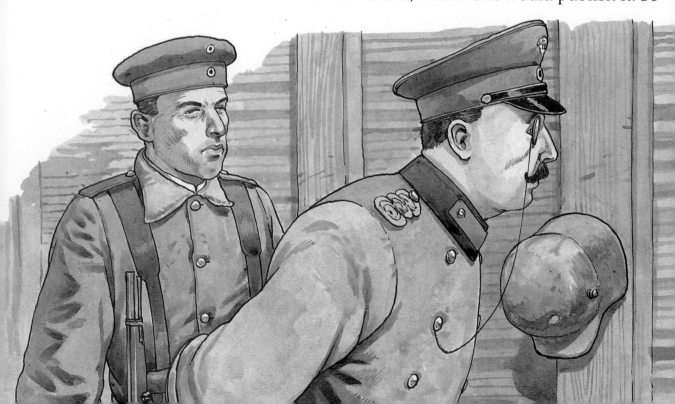

he paid the cost of publication himself. Support for his ideas came only from a few rocket enthusiasts. He learned of the work done by Robert Goddard in the U.S. and by Konstantin Tsiolkovski in Russia, and the three pioneers exchanged ideas by letter.

In 1929, Oberth's book *Way to Space Travel* predicted interplanetary flights by ion-engined rockets (a new concept not investigated until the 1960s). However, in the 1930s, only a few people considered the idea worthy of serious consideration.

World War II took Oberth to the German V2 rocket plant at Peenemunde. During the war, he designed the world's first surface-to-air guided missile.

After Germany's defeat in 1945, Oberth continued to design rockets in Switzerland and Italy, and from 1955 to 1958 in the U.S. He retired to Germany to write and lecture, and he lived to see many of his dreams come true: astronauts circling the Earth and walking on the surface of the Moon.

| | |
|---|---|
| **1894** | born at Hermannstadt, Transylvania (now part of Romania) |
| **1913** | student at Munich University |
| **1914** | World War I begins |
| **1923** | publishes *The Rocket into Interplanetary Space* |
| **1929** | writes *Way to Space Travel* |
| **1938** | becomes German citizen |
| **1939** | World War II begins |
| **1941** | works on V2 long-range missile |
| **1943** | works on anti-aircraft missiles |
| **1955** | designs rockets for U.S. Army |
| **1958** | retires to West Germany |

*Oberth's rocket designs impressed his commanding officer, but the German War Ministry considered his ideas too far-fetched to be taken seriously.*

11

# 4

# Wernher von Braun

Wernher von Braun once wrote that "science by itself has no moral dimension." In other words, science could not be good or bad – only the people who employed it could. Von Braun's career as a rocket engineer began in the 1930s, when, as a young physics graduate, he built small, liquid-fueled rockets. His career reached a climax in the 1960s in the U.S. with the Apollo Moon program. In between came his work at Peenemunde on the German V2 "revenge weapon."

From his early childhood, von Braun dreamed of space travel. Inspired (and baffled) by Oberth's vision of rockets in space, von Braun studied until he himself became a brilliant engineer. In the late 1930s, he and General Walter Dornberger were put in charge of the secret missile plant at Peenemunde. Von Braun designed the V2 rocket that bombarded Britain during World War II. This, and the other missiles

**1912** born Wirsitz, Germany (now in Poland)
**1925** reads Oberth's book *The Rocket into Interplanetary Space*
**1930** joins German Society for Space Travel
**1934** studies physics at Berlin University and carries out secret rocket tests
**1939** during World War II designs V2 and other military rockets
**1945** Germany surrenders to the allies
**1952** becomes head of U.S. Army missile program
**1955** U.S. citizenship granted
**1958** launches first U.S. satellite, Explorer 1
**1969** sees his saturn rocket launch first Moon-landing mission
**1972** resigns from N.A.S.A.
**1977** dies

his team produced, gave Germany a huge lead in rocket development.

Von Braun's rockets could not prevent Germany from losing the war. In 1945 (with many of his team), he was whisked away to the United States. There, he continued his V2 work, laying the foundations for the U.S. Army ballistic missile force.

His main interest, however, remained the use of rockets for space travel. He was ready to launch a U.S. satellite as early as 1954, but the Russians beat the Americans to it with their 1957 Sputnik success. Von Braun went to work for the newly formed N.A.S.A. (the National Aeronautics and Space Administration) as director of the Marshall Space Flight Center in Huntsville, Alabama. His mighty Saturn 5 booster, then the most powerful rocket yet built, launched the first Apollo astronauts to the Moon in 1969.

As popular enthusiasm for space flight waned after Apollo, von Braun continued to urge governments to pursue space research.

*Von Braun's V2 missile was used during World War II. The German missile led the way for post-war rocket technology in both the U.S. and U.S.S.R.*

# 5

# Sergei Korolyov

Until his death in 1966, few people in the West had heard of Sergei Korolyov. Yet he was the leading figure behind Soviet successes in space. An aeronautical engineer by training, he had worked in the 1930s with the famous aircraft designer A. N. Tupolev. Then his interest had been awakened in rocketry and, with a small group of enthusiastic colleagues, he launched the Soviet Union's first liquid-fueled rocket in 1933.

Such rockets were puny by comparison with the German V2 missiles of World War II. Korolyov got a chance to examine captured V2s in 1945. From test-firing captured V2s at the Kasputin Yar test range, Korolyov moved on to design and build the first generation of Soviet long-range missiles. Because Soviet atomic bombs were bigger and less sophisticated than American weapons, larger rockets were needed to carry

*Korolyov's Vostok launch vehicle was more powerful than any rocket built in the U.S. before Saturn 5. Vostok carried the first cosmonauts safely into orbit.*

them. Ironically, this guaranteed that the Russians would take the lead in space. Their huge missiles were modified by Korolyov and his team into readymade launch vehicles for satellites and astronauts. The launch of Sputnik 1, the first Earth satellite, in 1957, caused a sensation, most notably in the U.S. which was relying on the lightweight and unreliable Vanguard rocket to spearhead its own space program.

More shocks were in store. Korolyov's mighty Vostock rocket carried Yuri Gagarin into orbit in 1961, and the Russians went on to establish a clear lead in the space race. Not until the Apollo Moon landings of 1969 onward did the U.S. catch up. By then, Korolyov was dead. He had worked around the clock, personally supervising every launch. He had established the main Soviet spaceflight centers, seen the cosmonaut corps grow, and laid the foundations for the continuing successes of the Soviet space program.

| | |
|---|---|
| **1906** | born in the Ukraine, U.S.S.R. |
| **1923** | joins local aero club, flying gliders |
| **1924** | graduates from Odessa Building Trades School |
| **1926** | studies aeronautics in Moscow |
| **1933** | helps build first Russian research rocket |
| **1941** | under "technical arrest" during World War II, working on military projects |
| **1947** | test fires captured German V2 missiles |
| **1953** | chief designer of ballistic missiles |
| **1957** | launch of Sputnik 1 |
| **1961** | launch of Vostok 1, carrying Yuri Gagarin |
| **1966** | dies |

# 6

# Robert Gilruth

The U.S. space program owes much to the leadership of Robert Rowe Gilruth, an engineer and administrator with a knack for picking the right person for the job.

Gilruth began his career in the 1930s as a government scientist, studying the flight characteristics of airplanes. In 1945, his interest turned to pilotless aircraft and missiles, and he also became involved in the quest to break the so-called "sound-barrier."

In 1958, a year after the Russians had shocked the world by launching Sputnik 1, Gilruth was named director of a group of scientists whose job was to put an American into space. This was the beginning of N.A.S.A., which was to dominate American space science during the next decade. It also consumed vast amounts of money, as the manned spaceflight program accelerated to catch up with and, for a time surpass, the Russians.

| | |
|---|---|
| **1918** | born in Minnesota |
| **1936** | graduates with a degree in aeronautical engineering |
| **1945** | works on missile research at Wallops Island test range |
| **1947** | Bell X-1 rocket plane breaks the sound barrier |
| **1958** | appointed to head Mercury project |
| **1961** | director of Manned Spacecraft Center |
| **1962** | first American in space: John Glenn |
| **1969** | first American on Moon: Neil Armstrong |
| **1972** | named among first ten members of the National Space Hall of Fame |
| **1973** | steps down as N.A.S.A. boss |
| **1983** | retires from N.A.S.A. |

From humble beginnings, (a sub-orbital "hop" by astronaut Alan B. Shepard in 1961), N.A.S.A. progressed dramatically. John Glenn's three orbits in 1962 were the prelude to a string of successes with the Mercury spacecraft and the much larger Gemini. Gilruth became director of the Manned Spacecraft Center at Houston, Texas. "Mission Control" was the focal point of world news attention during the exciting build-up to the Apollo Moon landing of 1969.

Under Gilruth's direction, the U.S. sent six manned missions to the Moon. Following the last, by Apollo 17 in 1972, three missions to the Skylab space station were flown before Gilruth left his post in 1973. His N.A.S.A. career spanned the most adventurous and successful years of the American space program. In 1974, Robert Rowe Gilruth was elected to the U.S. National Academy of Sciences. It was just one of many honors he received for his part in putting Americans in space and on the Moon.

*Gilruth and his colleagues at Mission Control celebrate a successful splashdown. The Apollo Moon flights were a great achievement for the N.A.S.A. team.*

# 7

# Yuri Gagarin

Yuri Gagarin's place in history is assured. He was the first person to fly in space. His single orbit of the Earth on April 12, 1961, lasted only 108 minutes, yet the impact was enormous. This stocky Soviet fighter pilot suddenly became an international hero overnight.

Gagarin's school days were interrupted by the German invasion of Russia during World War II. After the war, however, the youthful Gagarin went to work in a foundry, studying science in evening classes. He went to a vocational college and got an aviation cadetship, hoping to make a career in the Soviet Air Force.

In 1957, Gagarin volunteered for a tour of duty in the Arctic. In 1959, he successfully applied to join the top-secret cosmonaut team being trained in a bid to gain for the Soviet Union the prize of launching the first person into space in 1961.

Gagarin's flight went smoothly. Strapped inside the spacecraft, he was launched into orbit

**1934** born in Klushino, U.S.S.R.
**1950** starts work in a foundry
**1951** attends Saratov technical school
**1955** air cadet at Orenburg Pilot Training School
**1957** joins Soviet Air Force and becomes a fighter pilot
**1960** accepted as one of the first group of Soviet cosmonauts
**1961** first flight on board Vostok 1 spacecraft
**1963** promoted to cosmonaut commander
**1966** loses active flight status
**1968** killed in plane crash

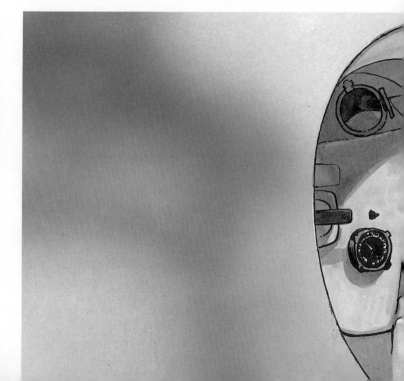

by a huge rocket. One orbit of the earth, a breathtaking first view of the planet from space, and it was over – ending in a parachute descent on Soviet territory, and a hero's welcome. He was later presented with many awards and honors.

Modestly, Gagarin accepted his sudden fame and assured people that he was anxious to return to space. He was spoken of as a future commander of a Soviet Moon mission. In 1966–7, he was preparing for a flight in the new Soyuz spacecraft, but the tragic death of fellow-cosmonaut Vladimir Komarov in 1967 halted the Soviet launch program.

Shortly afterward, Gagarin lost his active flight status. He may have been thought too valuable to risk following Komarov's accident. Some reports suggest that he was unfit, following a car accident. Whatever the reason, he was ordered to take a "refresher" course in flying. On March 27, 1968, he took off with another pilot in a MiG–15 trainer. The plane crashed 12 minutes later. Gagarin's body was never found.

**Above** *Yuri Gagarin as a student at the flying club.*

**Below** *Gagarin boarding the spacecraft for his historic flight.*

# 8

# John Glenn

On February 20, 1962, John Herschel Glenn became the first American to orbit the Earth. As one of the first pioneers of space travel, he was appropriately named, after British astronomer Sir John Herschel (1792–1871). His small spacecraft was called *Friendship 7*, and it was launched on top of a hastily converted Atlas rocket.

John Glenn was one of the seven original astronauts selected in 1959 for the Mercury project. He had an engineering degree and, like the others, he was a pilot with thousands of hours' flying experience. Glenn had served as a Marine Corps fighter pilot during both World War II and the Korean War. In 1957, he set a record time flying across the U.S. in an F8 Crusader jet.

The United States had been taken aback by the Russian space "firsts," especially the historic flight by Yuri Gagarin in April, 1961. The U.S. responded by launching Mercury astronauts

**Below** *The F8 Crusader jet which Glenn flew across the U.S.*

Alan Shepard and Virgil Grissom on sub-orbital "hops" using small Redstone rockets. No civilian American rocket could match the Russian Vostok booster, so the Air Force's more powerful Atlas rocket was chosen for Glenn's flight. Despite many development problems, the Atlas proved a reliable launcher for the two-ton Mercury capsule.

Glenn was launched from Cape Canaveral in Florida and made three orbits of the Earth before landing safely in the Atlantic. His flight lasted less than five hours. N.A.S.A. had decided to end American manned flights with splashdowns at sea, with the capsule descending by parachute. The Russians have always brought their spacecraft down on land.

Glenn's flight proved to be his only space mission, although other Mercury astronauts went on to fly in larger spacecraft. Glenn remained with the space program until 1964, working on the Apollo project. A national hero after his morale-boosting flight, he later became a U.S. Senator.

**Above** *John Glenn in front of the Atlas rocket that launched Mercury into space.*

| | |
|---|---|
| **1921** | born Ohio |
| **1943** | joins U.S. Marine Corps |
| **1948** | serves as flying instructor |
| **1950** | Korean War, fighter pilot until war ends |
| **1956** | assigned to design new fighters in Washington |
| **1957** | sets transcontinental speed record |
| **1959** | selected for Project Mercury |
| **1962** | becomes first American to orbit the Earth |
| **1964** | resigns from astronaut duties |
| **1965** | retires from U.S. Marines |
| **1974** | elected to U.S. Senate |
| **1984** | bids unsuccessfully to be Democratic presidential candidate |

# 9
# Valentina Tereshkova

There were no women among the original selection of U.S. and Soviet astronauts. Some scientists believed that the stresses of space flight would be too severe for women's bodies. Besides, there were very few suitably experienced women jet pilots. Soviet space achievements in the early 1960s had startled most Western experts. Their surprise in June, 1963, when the Russians announced that their sixth cosmonaut was a woman turned to incredulity when her identity and background were revealed.

The first spacewoman's name was Valentina Tereshkova. She was not a pilot, but a textile technologist working in a cotton mill. Apparently inspired by the deeds of Yuri Gagarin and the other pioneer Soviet cosmonauts, she had written to the Soviet government, asking for the opportunity to take part in the Soviet space program.

With three other women, she was summoned to Moscow for training. Just over a year later, after a crash course in the bewildering technology

**1937** born in Maslennikovo, U.S.S.R.
**1953** starts work in a tire factory
**1955** moves to work in a cotton mill
**1959** makes first parachute jump
**1962** begins training as a cosmonaut
**1963** launch date June 16 in Vostok 6 spacecraft. Her flight lasts less than 3 days. Marries Andrian Nikolayev.
**1964** daughter Alyonka born
**1969** graduates from military air academy; later promoted to Colonel-Engineer in the Soviet Air Force
**1974** elected to Presidium of Supreme Soviet
**1977** awarded U.N. Gold Medal of Peace

of space, she was ready. The launch date was June 16, 1963.

Tereshkova's spacecraft, Vostok 6, was not alone in orbit. The Russians launched another, Vostok 5, making it the first mission to have two manned craft in orbit at the same time. Tereshkova performed so well that her flight was extended beyond the 24 hours originally planned.

The flight demonstrated that women could cope as well as men with the demands of space flight. Apart from space sickness (which affects many astronauts), Tereshkova suffered no ill effects. Soon after her triumphant return to earth, she married Vostok 3 pilot Andrian Nikolayev. The birth of their daughter the following year proved that the human reproductive system was not damaged by space flight.

Although by nature shy, avoiding media attention, Valentina Tereshkova became a goodwill ambassador, representing the U.S.S.R. at international women's conferences. Other women would later make longer space flights, but hers was the unique honor of being first.

**Above** *Valentina Tereshkova, the first woman in space.*

**Below** *Only three years after her first parachute jump, Tereshkova was accepted for cosmonaut training.*

# 10
# Vladimir Komarov

Space flight claimed its first fatality in April, 1967, with the death of Soviet cosmonaut Vladimir Komarov. Others had died in ground accidents, but so far as is known, Komarov was the first person to be killed during a mission.

Komarov was an engineer and came from an intellectual background. He had been temporarily dropped from the Soviet cosmonaut team in 1963 when doctors found he had an irregular heartbeat. By coincidence, U.S. astronaut Donald Slayton suffered from the same problem. Both men overcame the medical hurdle and made it into space.

Having proved his fitness, Komarov made his first space flight in October, 1964. With his two companions, he flew for one day and 17 minutes in the world's first three-person spacecraft, Voskhod 1.

Because of his skill as a test pilot and engineer, Komarov was the obvious choice to test the new Soyuz spacecraft. Had Komarov been unable to

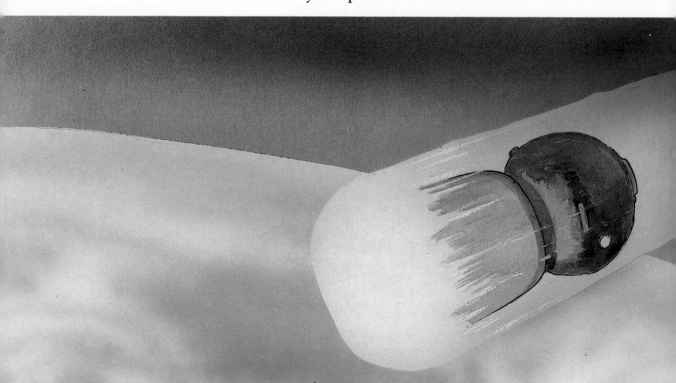

fly the Soyuz, backup pilot Yuri Gagarin would have stepped in.

When Komarov blasted off in the new spacecraft, he became the first cosmonaut to make a second flight. It is still not clear what went wrong. The official Soviet report describes how the Soyuz craft's parachute became entangled during its descent, sending the capsule crashing to the ground. However, radio transmissions picked up in the West seem to indicate that Komarov was in trouble much earlier. The Soyuz began to spin uncontrollably while in orbit. Ground control told Komarov to attempt re-entry, but both they and he must have known that the chances of a safe return were slim. The landing capsule apparently survived an uncontrolled plunge into the atmosphere, but Komarov was killed by the intense heat.

The disaster halted the Soyuz program for two years. As a tribute to the first man to die in space, one of the Soviet spacecraft-tracking ships is named *Cosmonaut Vladimir Komarov*.

| | |
|---|---|
| **1927** | born in Moscow, U.S.S.R. |
| **1942** | enters Moscow Air Force School |
| **1949** | joins Soviet Air Force as fighter pilot |
| **1954** | enters Zhukovsky Military Air Academy |
| **1959** | graduates as an engineer; assigned to research work |
| **1960** | selected as one of first group of cosmonauts. |
| **1962** | backup pilot for Vostok 4 mission |
| **1964** | rejoins cosmonauts after ill-health and commands three-man Voskhod 1 mission |
| **1966** | chief of Engineering Department at cosmonaut training center |
| **1967** | killed during re-entry of Soyuz 1 |

*Komarov's spacecraft overheated during re-entry into the atmosphere. But radio messages suggest the spacecraft was in trouble long before this.*

# 11
# Alexei Leonov

Could an astronaut survive, floating in the near-vacuum of space, beyond the protection of a spacecraft? No one knew for sure until 1965, when Soviet cosmonaut Alexei Leonov made the first E.V.A., or space "walk."

Leonov had a reputation among his comrades as a lucky daredevil. Several times in his life, he had escaped serious injury or death – once in an automobile accident, again when his parachute got tangled during a practice jump. He was much admired for his physical fitness, lively mind, and sense of humor. For some time, he was apparently favorite to make the first Soviet manned space flight. He had an even greater ambition: to be the first person on the Moon.

As it turned out, Leonov had to wait. He became the eleventh Russian to go into space. He never got to the Moon, for the Soviet Moon-landing program was abandoned. Nevertheless, he earned his place in space history. In March,

**Below** *Leonov's E.V.A. in 1965 was little more than a stunt. But it did demonstrate that astronauts could "walk" and work in space.*

1965, during his first space flight, he spent 24 minutes outside the Voskhod 2 craft. Predictably, things went wrong, and he had difficulty getting back on board. On their return, Leonov and co-pilot Pavel Belyaev landed far away from the planned target zone. Their capsule "landed" wedged between two fir trees amid deep snow. They had to wait 2½ hours before being rescued.

Unperturbed, Leonov went on to command the Soviet half of the 1975 Apollo-Soyuz Test Project. This was a joint flight, and docking took place in July, 1975. Leonov presented the American astronauts with drawings of themselves, done in his spare time during the space flight. He was an accomplished artist.

After this five-day mission, in Soyuz 19, Alexei Leonov retired from active space flight. He became deputy head of the Soviet cosmonaut training center. "Sad though it may be," he told reporters, "I am now a space veteran." However, he remained at work on the Soviet space program into the 1980s.

**Above** *Alexei Leonov (right) with U.S. astronaut Donald K. Slayton during the Apollo-Soyuz mission.*

| | |
|---|---|
| **1934** | born at Listvyanka, U.S.S.R. |
| **1945** | family moves to Kaliningrad |
| **1953** | leaves school for art college, but decides instead to join Air Force |
| **1957** | graduates from Air Force College |
| **1960** | selected for cosmonaut training |
| **1965** | first space flight, in Voskhod 2, and world's first "space walk" |
| **1975** | commands Soyuz 19 which docks with U.S. Apollo craft in orbit |

# 12
# Virgil Grissom

Virgil Ivan Grissom, nicknamed "Gus," was the second American to fly in space. His Mercury capsule was fired on a sub-orbital trajectory by a Redstone rocket. Grissom's 16-minute flight was longer than that of his fellow astronaut, Alan B. Shepard, by a full minute. This was in July, 1961, as the U.S. struggled to catch up with the Russians, who had put the first astronaut, Yuri Gagarin, into orbit around the Earth that same year.

Grissom was one of the seven original Mercury astronauts selected in 1959. As an Air Force colonel, he had flown jet fighters in the Korean War and later flew as a test pilot. He loved outdoor pursuits: hunting, fishing, skiing, and boating. Grissom's fondness for water was sorely tried when he landed in the Atlantic. His Mercury capsule sank as he was being picked up.

In March, 1965, Grissom flew a three-orbit mission as command pilot aboard Gemini 3 –

**Below** *Grissom's Mercury capsule sank when it landed in the ocean, but Grissom was saved by a helicopter.*

America's first two-person spacecraft. During the four-hour flight, he and co-pilot John Young carried out the first spacecraft maneuvers. Mastery of these techniques was essential if in-flight docking of two space vehicles was to be achieved.

American ambitions were set firmly on the Moon. Testing of the Apollo mooncraft began, and Grissom was chosen to pilot Apollo 1. But disaster struck in January, 1967, during a ground test. Grissom and his crew (Edward White and Roger Chaffee) were inside the spacecraft, running through a full-scale launch simulation when a flash fire broke out. The hatch could not be opened in time, and all three died.

The tragic accident was the worst until then in N.A.S.A.'s history. Design changes were made to the Apollo spacecraft, and it was October, 1968, before the first manned flight, Apollo 7, could be launched. Within a year, Apollo astronauts were standing on the Moon – the goal for which Grissom, White and Chaffee had given their lives.

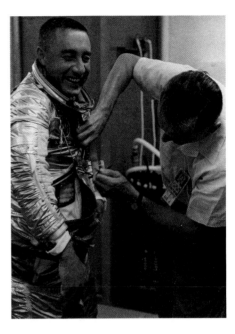

**Above** *Grissom jokes with a spacesuit specialist as he prepares for the second manned American space flight in 1961.*

| | |
|---|---|
| **1926** | born in Indiana |
| **1951** | gets a degree in engineering; qualifies as Air Force pilot |
| **1952** | returns to instructor duties after combat flying in Korea |
| **1955** | studies aeronautical engineering |
| **1957** | test pilot on fast jets |
| **1959** | selected for astronaut training |
| **1961** | sub-orbital flight, as second U.S. space flier |
| **1965** | command pilot of Gemini 3 |
| **1967** | dies in spacecraft fire at Cape Canaveral |

# 13
# James Lovell

Jim Lovell's career as a N.A.S.A. astronaut took him into space on four occasions, and his experiences are unique in the history of space exploration.

An experienced test pilot, Lovell joined N.A.S.A. in 1962. On his first space mission, in December, 1965, he and Frank Borman set a duration record in Gemini 7. His second space flight was in November, 1966, with Edwin Aldrin, aboard Gemini 12. On this, the last Gemini mission, Aldrin worked outside the spacecraft for more than five hours.

In December, 1968, Lovell and Borman joined forces again. With fellow crewman William Anders, they reached the highest speed ever attained by humans as Apollo 8 was blasted on its way to the Moon. It was the first time astronauts had ventured beyond Earth orbit. As

**Below** *James Lovell and the crew of Apollo 13 preparing the lunar landing module to make an emergency return to Earth after their Moon mission was aborted.*

Apollo 8 orbited the Moon ten times, the three Americans had a unique first view of the lunar surface from close range and of our own planet, seen from distant space.

In April, 1970, Lovell commanded Apollo 13, scheduled to make the third lunar landing. However, on the outward journey, there was an explosion in the service module of the Apollo craft. The mission was aborted, and Lovell and his crew transferred to the cramped lunar landing module. Carefully conserving precious power, water, and air supplies, they stayed there while the crippled spacecraft circled the Moon and returned to Earth. Just before re-entry into the Earth's atmosphere, the astronauts returned to the command module, (the only part of the Apollo craft able to return to Earth). Only the expertise of the crew and ground controllers allowed the spacecraft to land safely home.

**Above** *The crew of Apollo 8 prepare for simulated flight tests.*

| | |
|---|---|
| **1928** | born Ohio |
| **1952** | graduates from U.S. Naval Academy |
| **1958** | qualifies as test pilot |
| **1962** | selected for astronaut training |
| **1965** | first space flight, in Gemini 7 |
| **1966** | commander of Gemini 12 |
| **1968** | pilot and navigator of Apollo 8, flying around the Moon |
| **1970** | commander of Apollo 13, returning to Earth safely after Moon voyage abandoned |
| **1973** | retires from space program |

# 14
# Neil Armstrong

The two best-known names in space exploration are those of Yuri Gagarin (the first person to fly in space) and Neil Armstrong (the first person to set foot on the Moon).

Neil Alden Armstrong, aeronautical engineer and test pilot, joined the American space program in 1962. He was the first civilian astronaut in the U.S. His space baptism came in 1966 as command pilot of the two-man Gemini 8 spacecraft. This brief flight (only 10 hours) achieved an important first: a manually-controlled docking with another spacecraft.

President John Kennedy had vowed the U.S. would send astronauts to the Moon before the 1960s ended. By 1969, the Apollo team were ready to fulfill that vow. An outstandingly cool and skillful pilot, Armstrong was chosen ahead of more experienced astronauts to command N.A.S.A.'s first Moon flight. Launch date was July 16, 1969.

**1930** born Ohio
**1949** serves in U.S. Navy as pilot
**1952** studies aeronautical engineering
**1955** joins aeronautics research center as a test pilot
**1962** selected as a N.A.S.A. astronaut
**1966** first space flight, aboard Gemini 8
**1969** Apollo 11 lunar landing mission. Is the first person to walk on the Moon
**1971** leaves N.A.S.A. to become professor of aerospace engineering
**1980** moves from university to business career
**1986** vice-chairman of commission investigating *Challenger* disaster

Aboard the Apollo 11 spacecraft with Armstrong were Edwin Aldrin and Michael Collins. Once in orbit around the Moon, Armstrong and Aldrin transferred to the lunar module, code-named Eagle, while Collins remained in the command module. The lunar module flew down to land in the Sea of Tranquillity. On July 20 at 8.17 p.m, Armstrong clambered down the ladder to stand on the powdery surface of the Moon. His first words, "That's one small step for a man, one giant leap for mankind," passed into history.

Together, Armstrong and Aldrin spent 21½ hours on the Moon, before returning in the lunar module to rejoin Collins, waiting patiently in orbit. Apollo 11 returned to Earth with more than 46 pounds (21 kg) of lunar rock and soil samples. Millions of people on earth watched on television as each stage of this historic first exploration of another world was enacted.

For Armstrong, there were to be no further space adventures. He resigned from N.A.S.A. to teach engineering at the University of Cincinnati. In 1986, he served on the commission that investigated the *Challenger* space shuttle accident.

*Neil Armstrong and Edwin Aldrin on the Moon. Armstrong is collecting a sample of lunar rock, while Aldrin sets up a solar wind experiment.*

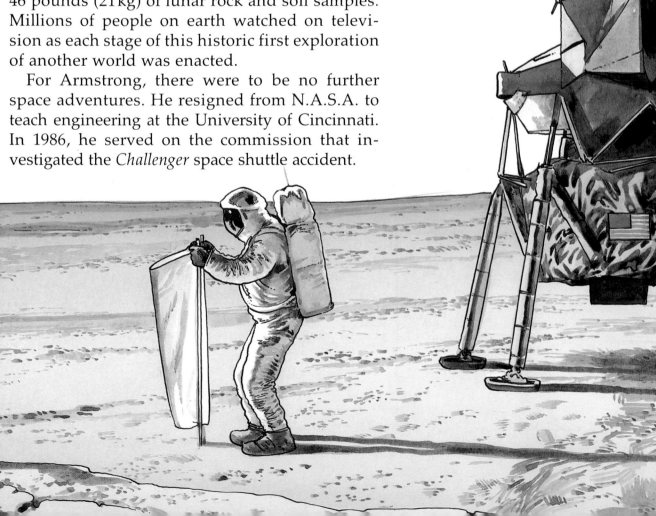

# 15

# John Young

American space veteran John Young was the first to complete six space flights. His career spanned the history of America's space flight program, from the two-man Gemini capsule to the space-shuttle, the world's first re-usable spacecraft.

Like many other American astronauts, John Young was a former military test pilot. He clocked up more the 11,000 hours flying time, including 835 hours in space. He began his space career with fellow-astronaut Gus Grissom, testing the first Gemini craft in 1965. In 1966, he commanded Gemini 10, which carried out docking experiments in Earth orbit. In 1969, in Apollo 10, Young orbited the Moon in the command module while below, testing the lunar module, astronauts Tom Stafford and Eugene Cernan had a tantalizingly close view of the lunar landscape from a height of 9½ miles (15 km).

John Young landed on the Moon in April, 1972,

**Below** *John Young using the battery-powered lunar roving vehicle to explore the Moon in 1972.*

as commander of Apollo 16, the last-but-one Moon landing. He and Charlie Duke explored the rugged lunar highlands and drove more than 16½ miles (27km) in a lunar rover vehicle.

His fifth and sixth flights were both in the space shuttle. In April, 1981, Young commanded the first flight of the orbiter Columbia, which made 36 Earth orbits before gliding back to land at Edwards Air Force Base in California. In December, 1983, Young was back in space again, as commander of the first shuttle to carry Spacelab (a science laboratory carried in the spacecraft's cargo bay).

During this 10-day mission, Young and his five crew members worked 12-hour shifts, producing more technical data than all previous Apollo and Skylab missions put together.

John Young is still a key figure at N.A.S.A. He was Chief of the Astronaut Office until 1987, and thereafter an adviser on the future of the shuttle program. He is also involved in plans for a new generation of spacecraft.

**Above** *Spacecraft commander John Young gives a thumbs-up "OK" during training for the first launch of the space shuttle* Columbia *in 1981.*

| | |
|---|---|
| **1930** | born San Francisco |
| **1952** | degree in aeronautical engineering |
| **1959** | qualifies as naval test pilot |
| **1962** | selected for astronaut training |
| **1965** | first flight, Gemini 3 (first American two-man spacecraft) |
| **1966** | Gemini 10 flight, with Michael Collins |
| **1969** | Apollo 10 (rehearsal for Moon landing) |
| **1972** | Moon landing, in Apollo 16 |
| **1974** | becomes Chief of Astronaut Office |
| **1981** | first shuttle test |
| **1983** | first Spacelab mission |
| **1987** | special assistant to Director of Johnson Space Center, Houston |

# 16
# Valery Ryumin

Soviet cosmonaut Valery Ryumin has spent almost a year of his life in space. Moreover, at 6'3" (1.92 m), he disproves the idea that only short people are chosen for space flight. (It may have been true in the 1960s, when spacecraft were smaller.)

Unusually among Soviet cosmonauts, Siberian-born Ryumin was a soldier, not an Air Force pilot. When he joined the cosmonauts in 1973, he had been a civilian engineer for twelve years. He was an expert in electronics. His work on the Salyut space station helped to give the U.S.S.R. its lead in long-stay manned missions. The reliable Salyut-Soyuz combination worked well throughout the 1970s and 1980s.

Valery Ryumin first flew in space in Soyuz 25, launched in October, 1977. Ironically, this was one of the few occasions when things went

*Soyuz 32 moves in to dock with the Salyut 6 space station.*

wrong. The docking system failed, and Soyuz had to return without linking up with the Salyut 6 station. The failure weighed heavily on Ryumin, and he was anxious to try again.

In February, 1979, his chance came. He flew as flight engineer in Soyuz 32. The craft docked with Salyut 6, and Ryumin and his partner, Vladimir Lyakhov, stayed in space for over 175 days.

Only months after his return, he went into space again, on board Soyuz 35, for another long stay on Salyut 6. His intimate knowledge of the Salyut systems made him the best choice as stand-in for an injured colleague, Valentin Lebedev. With pilot Leonid Popov, Ryumin established a new duration record – 184 days in space. Cosmonauts visiting them during their six-month stay included a Hungarian, a Vietnamese, and a Cuban. Within two days of landing, Ryumin, the dedicated engineer, was testing his own body – by playing tennis.

| | |
|---|---|
| **1939** | born in Siberia, U.S.S.R. |
| **1957** | graduates from technical college and joins the Red Army |
| **1961** | studies electronics and computing before joining the Korolyov spacecraft design bureau |
| **1973** | selected for cosmonaut training |
| **1977** | first space flight, aboard Soyuz 25 |
| **1979** | second space flight, aboard Soyuz 32 |
| **1980** | third flight, aboard Soyuz 35; sets endurance record |
| **1983** | flight director for later Soviet missions |

# 17
# Rakesh Sharma

Most of the people who have flown in space have been either Americans or Russians, since so far only the U.S.A. and the U.S.S.R. have launched manned spacecraft. However, through their Intercosmos program, begun in 1978, the Russians offered cosmonauts from other countries the chance to fly alongside Soviet crews. Rakesh Sharma became the first Indian cosmonaut.

Major Sharma was the younger of two Indian Air Force test pilots selected for astronaut training after the Russian invitation. His companion was Lieutenant-Colonel Ravish Malhotra. Malhotra was chosen as one of the prime flight crew, with Sharma as part of the backup, or reserve crew.

The two Indian pilots journeyed to the Soviet space training center in Star Town near Moscow. The harsh Russian winter was an extra hardship on top of the rigorous cosmonaut training.

**Below** *Rakesh Sharma and a fellow cosmonaut carrying out experiments using plants and insects aboard a space station.*

Luckily, Rakesh is a good linguist, so he found learning Russian fairly easy. This skill earned him an unexpected promotion. The Soviet mission controllers decided that since his Russian was more fluent, Sharma should replace Malhotra and make the flight aboard the Soyuz T-11.

The launch date was April 3, 1984. All went smoothly, and the Soyuz docked with the orbiting Salyut 7 space station. Sharma and his fellow astronauts transferred to Salyut and were greeted by its three-man crew. For the next few days, Sharma was kept busy with scientific work, carrying out experiments for Indian and Soviet scientists. He also performed yoga exercises to see what effect they had on space-sickness. After a flight lasting 7 days, 21 hours, and 41 minutes, Soyuz returned to Earth.

Sharma's achievement was recognized in both the U.S.S.R. and in India, where there was great pride at his success. He later returned to his career as a test pilot.

**Above** *The flags of India and the U.S.S.R. are displayed behind the cosmonauts who took part in the Soviet-India mission.*

| | |
|---|---|
| **1949** | born in Patiala, Punjab, India |
| **1966** | graduates from Nizam College in Hyderabad; joins Indian Air Force as cadet |
| **1971** | flies MiG fighters during Bangladesh war |
| **1972** | qualifies as test pilot |
| **1979** | U.S.S.R. invites India to join Intercosmos program |
| **1981** | joins astronaut selection group |
| **1982** | begins training with Soviet cosmonauts in the U.S.S.R. |
| **1983** | chosen to make Soyuz T–11 flight |
| **1984** | spends over a week in orbit, becoming the first person from a non-aligned (neutral) country to fly in space |

# 18
# Sally Ride

The first American woman to fly in space commented afterward that it was "no big deal." According to Sally Ride, the media attention her June, 1983, space flight received simply showed that women were still not accepted, without comment, as being able to do the same work as men.

Sally Kristen Ride was no token female among the N.A.S.A. astronauts. She was an astrophysicist from Stanford University, California, who joined the astronaut team in 1978 as one of a new generation of mission specialists. A year of training confirmed her assignment to a future space shuttle mission.

Only two women had flown in space before Ride: Valentina Tereshkova and Svetlana Savitskaya of the U.S.S.R. Sally Ride's first shuttle mission began with the launch of STS–7 from the Kennedy Space Center, Florida. It was the second flight of the orbiter vehicle *Challenger* and the

| | |
|---|---|
| **1951** | born in California |
| **1973** | first degrees in physics and English |
| **1978** | doctorate in physics from Stanford University: selected as one of 35 astronaut candidates |
| **1979** | assigned to shuttle program |
| **1983** | first flight in *Challenger* |
| **1984** | second flight, also in *Challenger* |
| **1985** | assigned to third space flight |
| **1986** | *Challenger* disaster halts shuttle program |
| **1987** | leaves N.A.S.A. to return to university life |

first shuttle mission to carry a five-person crew. During the six-day flight in Earth orbit, Ride helped to launch two commercial satellites for Canada and Indonesia. She also carried out tests with the shuttle's remote manipulator system.

In October, 1984, Sally Ride flew her second mission, STS 41–G, again on board *Challenger*. Seven astronauts (a record number) traveled on this shuttle mission.

The shuttle program seemed to be going well. Sally Ride was preparing for a third mission when tragedy hit. In January, 1986, *Challenger* blew up shortly after launch. All seven astronauts on board died instantly. Subsequent shuttle flights were suspended for almost three years. Ride served on the commission inquiring into the accident.

In 1987, Sally Ride left N.A.S.A. to resume her academic career. She returned to Stanford, to work as a physicist at the University's center for international security and arms control.

**Above** *Sally Ride talks to ground control by radio during the seventh shuttle mission in June, 1983.*

**Below** *The open cargo bay of the shuttle. Ride has carried out experiments on the shuttle's remote manipulator system.*

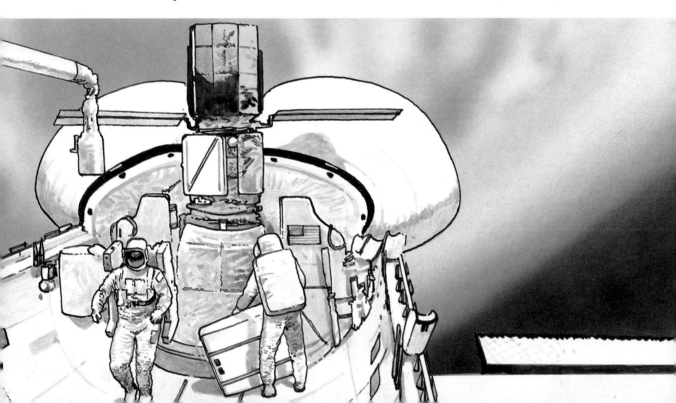

# 19
# Yuri Romanenko

On December 29, 1987, a Soyuz TM-3 space capsule landed in Soviet Kazakhstan, and from it emerged Yuri Romanenko. He had spent the previous 326 days in space, a new record. Romanenko had lived and worked in the Mir space station, the successor to the well-tried Salyut. During his long stay in weightlessness, he had grown taller by half an inch (one of the unexpected physiological effects of prolonged space flight). Despite regular workouts on a treadmill and an exercise bike, his calf muscles had shrunk by 15 percent. Doctors are concerned about the physical and mental stresses on men and women undertaking long space flights. A Mars voyage, the ultimate target, would last more than two years.

Romanenko's first space flight was in 1977 aboard Soyuz 26. During this flight, he made a space "walk" without checking that his safety line was secured and nearly floated away into space. He

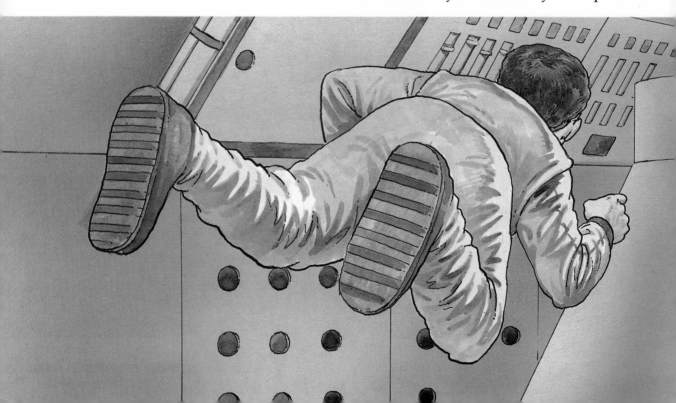

was saved by his partner, Georgi Grechko, who grabbed the free end of the line just in time.

After this 96-day flight, Romanenko took part in a joint Soviet-Cuban mission aboard Soyuz 38 in 1980. This flight lasted just over a week. He then had to wait until 1987 for his next space flight, the record-breaking endurance test aboard Mir. Even as he and two fellow-cosmonauts left the space station, a replacement crew of two men were settling in for an even longer stay.

The Soviets have achieved the goal they have striven toward ever since they abandoned hopes of beating the United States to the Moon. They can maintain a space station in orbit, resupplying it from Earth using unmanned space "freighters." By exchanging crews regularly, they will be able to keep such stations permanently manned. Without such flights as Yuri Romanenko's, and intensive medical studies of cosmonauts in space and on Earth, we shall not know if manned voyages to Mars and beyond will be possible.

| | |
|---|---|
| **1944** | born at Koltubanovsky, U.S.S.R. |
| **1962** | joins the Soviet Air Force |
| **1966** | graduates as an engineer-pilot instructor |
| **1969** | selected for cosmonaut training |
| **1975** | ground crew for U.S. Soviet ASTP flight |
| **1977** | first space flight in Soyuz 26 |
| **1980** | commander of Soyuz 38, with Cuban companion, docks with Salyut space station |
| **1987** | record-breaking 326-day flight, visiting new Mir space station |

*Romanenko and other long-stay cosmonauts exercise in space to keep themselves fit enough to do their work.*

43

# 20
# Carl Sagan

Astrophysicist Carl Sagan is one of the world's best-known scientists, largely because of his ability as a communicator. In the 1960s, his experiments re-created in the laboratory the conditions under which life on Earth may have begun many millions of years ago. He studied our neighboring planets, Mars and Venus, and worked on the U.S. program to send space probes to map and eventually land on Mars.

The 1976 *Viking* landers found no evidence of life on Mars. However, like other scientists, Sagan sees no reason to suppose that Earth is the only planet in the vast Universe that is able to support life. In books such as *The Cosmic Connection*, he explored the possibility that one day humans may make contact with alien civilizations in far distant galaxies.

Sagan pointed out that human history is

fleeting, in cosmic terms. His "cosmic calendar" equates the age of the Universe with a single Earth year. The Universe begins with the "Big Bang" of creation on January 1. Life on earth does not appear until September; humans not until 10.30 p.m. of the very last day of the year.

The *Pioneer* and *Voyager* space probes already launched from Earth will in time travel far beyond our galaxy. The spacecraft carry simple coded messages explaining their origins – in case aliens should ever come across them. In his books and in television series such as *Cosmos* (1980), Carl Sagan has opened people's eyes and minds to the wonders of space. He has also warned of the dangers threatening our own planet. With other concerned scientists, Sagan has spoken of the risk of nuclear war and of a life-destroying "nuclear winter" that might follow. Such a self-inflicted catastrophe would wipe out our world, which appears to be unique in supporting life.

| | |
|---|---|
| **1934** | born New York City |
| **1966** | writes *Intelligent Life in the Universe* |
| **1968** | professor of astronomy and space sciences at Cornell University |
| **1969** | Mariner probes 6 and 7 fly by Mars |
| **1971** | Mariner 9 orbits Mars |
| **1972** | launch of Pioneer 10, first spacecraft to leave the solar system |
| **1974** | *The Cosmic Connections* published |
| **1976** | Viking spacecraft land on Mars |
| **1977** | awarded Pulitzer prize for *The Dragons of Eden*, a book about human intelligence |
| **1979** | Voyager probes launched |
| **1980** | presents *Cosmos* TV series |
| **1984** | warns of dangers of "nuclear winter" |

*The* Viking *lander on Mars in 1976. A robot arm scoops up samples of martian soil for biological testing. However, it found no evidence of life on Mars.*

# Glossary

**Apollo** Spacecraft used in American Moonflights from 1969 to 1972.

**ASTP** Apollo Soyuz Test Project, a joint American-Soviet mission in Earth orbit in 1975.

**Booster** Rocket engine that provides initial thrust for a launch and is then discarded.

**Cape Canaveral** Main American launch site, in Florida; formerly Cape Kennedy.

**Capsule** Small spacecraft, such as the early Vostok and Mercury vehicles.

**Docking** Joining up of two spacecraft in space.

**EVA** Extra-Vehicular Activity, or space "walk."

**Gemini** American two-man spacecraft first flown in 1965.

**Liquid fuels** Preferred to solid fuels for space rockets. The American Saturn 5 rocket burned a mixture of liquid oxygen and liquid hydrogen.

**Mercury** First American manned spacecraft.

**Module** Part of a spacecraft. The Apollo craft was made up of the command module, service module, and lunar module.

**Pioneer 10** First spacecraft to leave the solar system (1983), eleven years after launch by the U.S.

**Probe** Unmanned spacecraft sent to explore distant space and planets.

**Re-entry** When a spacecraft returns to Earth, as it passes through the atmosphere.

**Salyut** Soviet space station. First launched in 1971. Five further Salyuts launched to date.

**Saturn** American rocket designed by Wernher von Braun's team to send astronauts to the Moon.

**Skylab** Orbital space station visited by three crews of American astronauts during the 1970s.

**Soyuz** Soviet spacecraft first flown in 1967. More than 50 Soyuz vehicles have been launched subsequently.

**Space shuttle** Reusable spacecraft, first flown 1981. Flight program temporarily halted after 1986 accident when one of the four shuttle orbiters was destroyed.

**Splashdown** Landing a spacecraft in the sea.

**Sputnik** Russian word for "satellite."

**Star Town** Zvezdny Gorodok, near Moscow, the site of the Soviet cosmonaut training center where Soviet and foreign crews train for space flight.

**V2** German rocket missile fired against Britain during World War II.

**Viking** Unmanned spacecraft used in Mars landings (1976).

**Vostok** Soviet spacecraft used by first six Soviet cosmonauts.

**Voyager** Two *Voyager* probes launched in 1979 by the U.S. flew past Jupiter and Saturn, sending back the first close-up pictures of the planets.

**Wind tunnel** Device for testing aircraft designs in model form.

# Further reading

*How Did We Find Out about Outer Space?* by Isaac Asimov (Avon, 1981)

*Living in Space* by James S. Trefil (Macmillan, 1981)

*One Giant Leap for Mankind* by Carter Smith (Silver, Burdett & Ginn, 1986)

*Space Law* by Necia Apfel (Franklin Watts, 1988)

*Space: Battleground of the Future?* by L.B. Taylor, Jr. (Franklin Watts, 1988)

*Story of the Space Shuttle, The* by Tim Furniss (David & Charles, 1986)

*Voyager: The Story of a Space Mission* by Margaret Poynter & Arthur L. Lane (Macmillan, 1981)

# Index

## Picture acknowledgements

Photographs supplied by Camera Press 39; Science Photo Library 21, 23, 27, 29, 31, 35, 41;
Wayland Picture Library 9, 19.

Concora
South Side